Terrance Talks Travel:
The Quirky Tourist Guide to Charleston

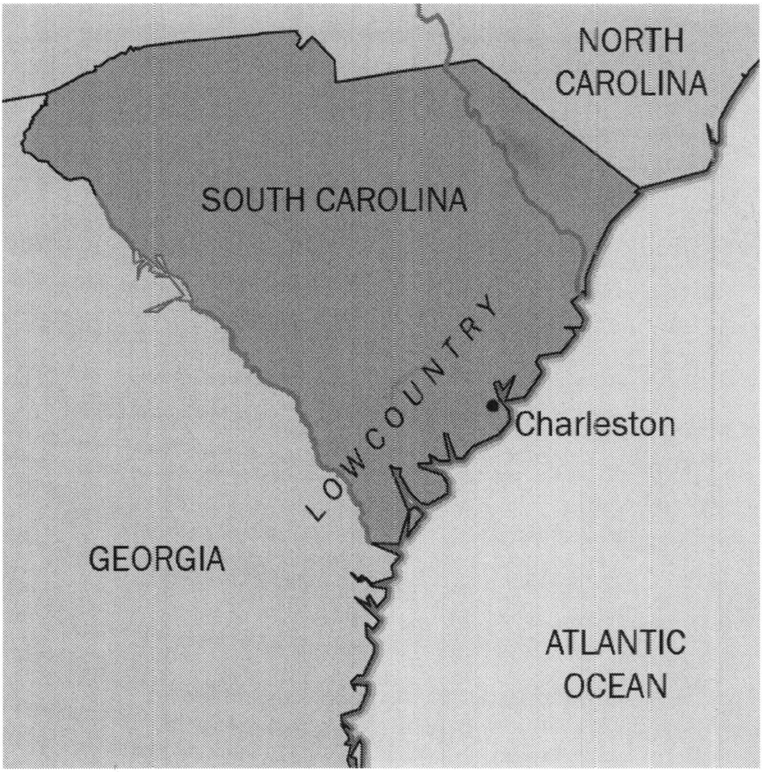

NORTH CAROLINA

SOUTH CAROLINA

LOWCOUNTRY

Charleston

GEORGIA

ATLANTIC OCEAN

Terrance Zepke

All queries should be directed to: www.safaripublishing.net.

For more about the author, www.terrancezepke.com and www.terrancetalkstravel.com.

ISBN-13: 978-1942738435
ISBN-10: 1942738439

Library of Congress Cataloging-in-Publication Data

America/Zepke, Terrance p. cm.

Terrance Talks Travel: The Quirky Tourist Guide to Charleston

1. Travel-South Carolina. 2. Travel-Southeast U.S. 3. Charleston. 4. Charleston Beaches. 5. South Carolina Lowcountry. 6. Charleston History & Folklore. 7. Charleston Guidebook. 9. Charleston Tours. 10. Charleston Attractions. I. Title.

First edition

Safari Publishing

CONTENTS

INTRODUCTION

I just have to say right up front that Charleston is my favorite town in America. I'll admit, I may be prejudice since I am from the South Carolina Lowcountry, but you don't have to take my word for it. Do a Google search and you'll see that the media and millions of visitors agree. Charleston has received every award imaginable, from "Prettiest Small Town" to "Best City in America". There is so much to see and do that you can only hope to skim the surface during your initial visit.

In fact, it took me twice as long to write this book as any book I've written in this series. The reason being that Charleston has so many historical sites (It is one of America's oldest cities), museums, festivals, activities, and tours. Charleston is also one of the most haunted cities in America, so there are lots of ghost walks and graveyard tours. What's more, there are several renowned beach resorts and barrier islands within a few minutes' drive from Charleston.

For those of you who scour the Internet before every trip searching for anything out of the ordinary, you won't have to look far this time. Charleston is full of charm and quirkiness. I'm going to show you authentic Charleston, which includes Gullah tours, Hoodoo, graveyard tours, shrimp shacks, pirates, and much more!

I also reveal the best rooftop bar, best place to go for dessert, best souvenir shop, best plantation, best beach resort, and more. Additionally, I'll share unique experiences with you, including spending the night on the *USS Yorktown*, attending flight academy, a store devoted exclusively to Moon pies®, the most unusual festival (even for South Carolina!), how you can participate in a paranormal investigation of one of Charleston's most haunted sites, and more.

One piece of advice I'd like to share is to plan ahead. Charleston is one of the most population destinations in America. The city gets more than eight million visitors a year. So if you want to participate in a particular festival or special event or visit during peak season, you need to make reservations as soon as possible. Only small groups are permitted for some tours and attractions, so that's another reason you should pre-book. I suggest making a list of your top five or ten things you want to do for sure during your visit. Then you should create a rough itinerary so you know when to make reservations and buy tickets. Make sure you understand refund policies in case you need to change or cancel a reservation.

If you are planning to visit other places in coastal South Carolina, you may want to get my book, *COASTAL SOUTH CAROLINA: WELCOME TO THE LOWCOUNTRY*. It discusses most of the South Carolina coast, including Charleston. This reference expands on that discussion and focuses on quirky tourism. It can be a companion guide or a stand-alone reference for those traveling exclusively to Charleston.

So read on to learn how to make the most out of your time in one of the most historic, charming, intriguing, haunted, and prettiest places in America. Be sure to pay special attention to my TOP TEN PICKS, Annual Events, and FYI boxes.

FYI: Something many folks like to do when visiting Charleston is to also visit beaches on nearby Sea Islands, such as Isle of Palms and Kiawah. In fact, some visitors choose to stay at one of these beach communities and drive into Charleston to explore, shop and dine. More information about these places can be found throughout this book.

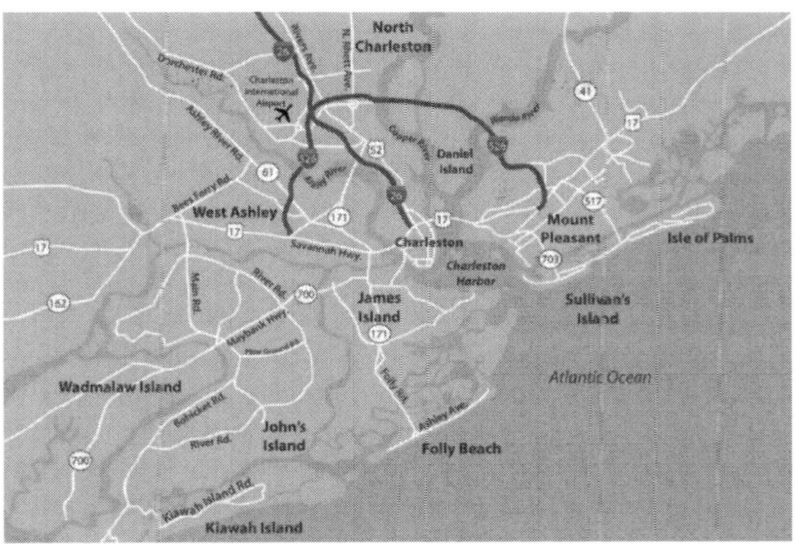

GETTING THERE

By Air

There is one airport, **Charleston International Airport** (CHS), which is located eleven miles northwest of historic downtown. All major and most regional airlines fly into CHS. Upon arrival, you can rent a car at the airport, take a CARTA city bus, an airport shuttle, and there is also the option to take a taxi.

FYI: There are (33) thirty-three major metropolitan areas within 350 miles of Charleston.

By Land

Charleston is in the middle of South Carolina's coastline. It can be reached from the north or south using Highway 17. From the west, travelers will use I-26, which ends northwest of downtown, where you will pick up Highway 17. If coming from the airport, you will use I-526 to reach Highway 17.

Distance from Charleston to...
Columbia, SC=110 miles
Charlotte, NC=209 miles
Atlanta, GA=291 miles
Orlando, FL=384 miles
Miami, FL=590 miles
Louisville, KY=620 miles
Memphis, TN=696 miles
Indianapolis, ID=726 miles
Chicago, IL=909 miles

The Arthur J Ravenel Bridge opened in 2005. It extends 1,546 feet over the Cooper. It is the longest cable stay span bridge in North America.

More Options

Amtrak has a station ten miles north of downtown. www.amtrak.com.

The **Greyhound Bus Station** is in North Charleston. To get to downtown Charleston, take the #11 bus, which stops across the street from the station. Ride it until you reach the last stop, which is the downtown Charleston Visitor's Center. www.greyhound.com.

The **ACE Basin Express** offers service between downtown Charleston and downtown Savannah. The bus departs from the Charleston Visitor's Center and Trade Center Landing in Savannah. There are pick-ups and drop-offs for area hotels. For those making a day trip from Savannah to Charleston or vice versa, this two-hour shuttle is the best option. You can leave the driving, navigating, and parking to someone else and just enjoy the scenic drive.
http://www.basinbus.com/

By Boat and Cruise Ship

Experienced boaters can reach this port city by private boat. There are many marinas in the Greater Charleston area. The website for the **Charleston City Marina** is http://www.charlestoncitymarina.com/ and for a complete list, https://marinas.com/browse/marina/US/SC/. Cruise ships depart regularly from the **Port of Charleston's Cruise Passenger Terminal**, http://www.scspa.com/getting-to-charleston/ for the Bahamas, Bermuda, and the Caribbean. If you are taking a cruise out of Charleston, you should allow at least two extra days to see the area sights before embarkation.

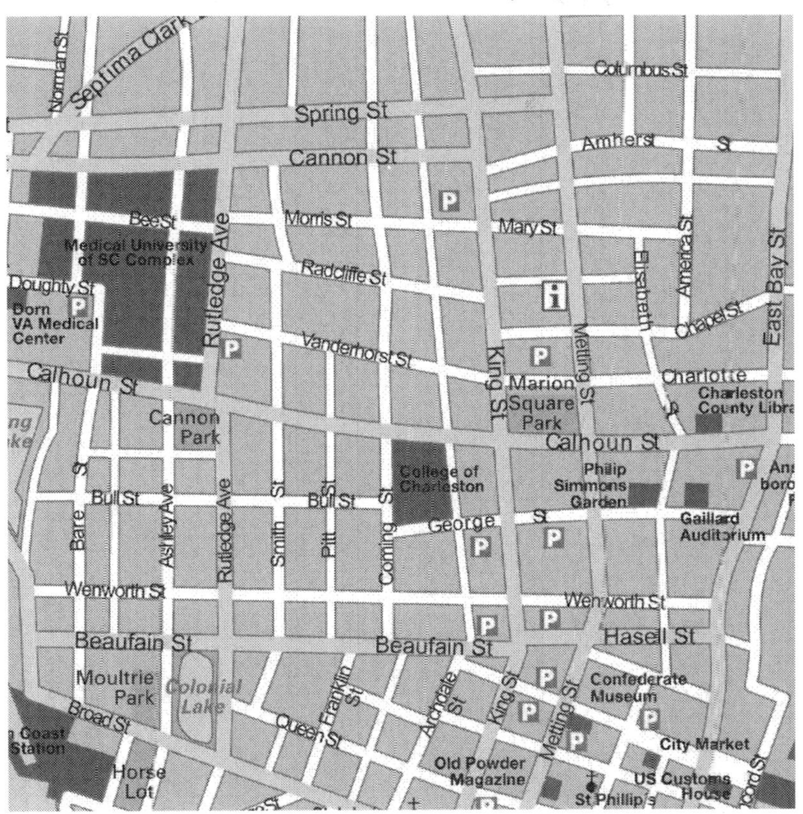

Getting Around Charleston

Parking is problematic in Charleston. There is limited metered street parking, and there is a parking garage at the visitor center, which fills out quickly in peak season. It is best to walk, take a taxi, arrange a tour, or hop on one of the city's trolleys. For sites outside of downtown Charleston, you will need to rent a car if you do not have your vehicle or take a day tour. Tour options are discussed in the Touristy Things to See and Do chapter.

FYI: To view fully navigable maps of greater Charleston, http://www.things-to-do-in-charleston.com/charleston-maps.html. Tickets to tours and attractions, hotel bookings, and maps and brochures can be purchased at the Charleston Area Visitor Center. Private tours of Charleston can be arranged with licensed tour guides, so ask if interested. 315 Meeting Street. http://www.charlestoncvb.com/travel-support/visitors-centers/

The streets in downtown in Charleston are more or less parallel and perpendicular to the waterfront. The major east-west street is **Calhoun Street**, and the major north-south street is **King Street**, which is the main shopping street in downtown Charleston.

Several blocks south is a major east-west street, **Broad Street**, which is known by locals as "North of Broad" and "South of Broad." Residents and businesses South of Broad are commonly dubbed SOB, and those Slightly North of Broad are SNOBs.

The French Quarter, founded by the French Huguenots, is just south of the Market Area along the waterfront. The area near the southern tip of the peninsula, where the Ashley and Cooper Rivers meet, is known as The Battery (pictured here).

Fast Facts:

Population: 135,000 Charleston and 396,484 for Charleston County
Area: 127.49 square miles (330.20 km)
Time Zone: Eastern Standard Time
Average Temperatures: 90◦F (32◦C) during summe and 60◦F during winter (16◦C); Overall Average=75◦F (24◦C); daily average humidity=73%
Language: While English commonly considered to be the only official language, 'Gullah' was proclaimed as an official language of Charleston in

1939. Variations of it are still spoken today along the South Carolina and Georgia coasts.

History: A flotilla of three small ships carrying 148 English men and women sailed into a harbor on the SC coast in April 1670 and established the settlement of Charles Town, named for England's King Charles II.

Historic District: Charleston's historic district boasts 2,000 preserved and restored buildings with more than 130 structures dating from the 1700s and 600 from the early 1800s. Roughly 70 buildings pre-date the Revolutionary War. Charleston's downtown extends nearly five miles.

Charleston architecture: The most common architectural styles are Federal, Georgian, Greek Revival, Italianate, and Queen Anne. Traditional Charleston homes and buildings have decks or piazzas that face south or west to best catch the breeze.

TERRANCE'S TOP TEN PICKS

1. **Walk the Museum Mile**. Along a one-mile stretch of Meeting Street, you can visit most of the city's historical highlights. This includes six museums, five historic houses, four scenic parks, a Revolutionary War Powder Magazine (South Carolina's oldest public building), and many houses of worship and public buildings, like the

Market and City Hall. http://www.charlestonsmuseummile.org/

Charleston She Crab Soup Recipe

Ingredients:

5 Tbsp. butter
1 Small Vidalia onion
1 Stalk celery, grated
2 Cloves garlic, minced
2 Quarts half-and-half cream
1 Pint heavy cream
1 cup chicken broth

A dash of Old Bay Seasoning
2 tsp Worcestershire sauce
1 pound lump crabmeat
1 Tbsp. Chives, chopped
salt and pepper to taste
Sherry (optional)

Melt butter over medium heat. Slowly stir in flour and cook for 2-3 minutes, stirring constantly. Add onion, celery, garlic, and salt and pepper. Cook for five minutes. Whisk cream and slowly add to pot. Stir in chicken broth. Bring to a simmer and add the rest of the ingredients, except for crabmeat, sherry, and chives. Cover and let simmer for 25-30 minutes, stirring occasionally. After reduction has occurred, add crabmeat and simmer for 5-10 minutes. Serve in soup bowls and top with a sprinkle of chives (or you can substitute parsley for the garnish). The sherry is optional but it does make the soup more flavorful, so I do recommend it. You don't taste the sherry (and you don't want to add but a wee bit), but it does enhance the soup. You should add a splash of sherry to each bowl, stir, and then garnish. This is a rich, creamy soup that looks and tastes more like a bisque than soup. *It is so good!*

FYI: The origin of she-crab soup dates back to the early 1900s. According to legend, President Taft was visiting Charleston's Mayor Rhett. The men were dining at the John Rutledge House when Mayor Rhett asked his butler to do something to their Partan-bree (a Scottish crab and rice dish) to make it fancier. The butler, an African-American named William Deas, added crab roe (crab eggs). Over the years, a few other additions have resulted in this being known as she-crab soup. A she crab has a wider abdomen plate than the male crab, which makes the meat better. Nowadays, it is hard to find she crabs, so blue crabs, regular crabs, and lump crabmeat are often substituted.

2. **Dig into some Lowcountry cuisine**. This is a dining adventure! Dare to try delicious Lowcountry staples, such as Okra Soup, Shrimp and Grits (pictured here), She Crab Soup, Benne Wafers, Frogmore Stew, Huguenot Torte, Chicken Bog, Sweet Potato Pone, and more. There are lots of good places to go in Charleston (and don't worry, I go into this more in depth in my BEST OF CHARLESTON chapter). But I think the best place for visitors is **Hominy Grill**. This award-winning eatery serves breakfast, lunch, brunch, and dinner. This Charleston landmark is a great place to meet locals and taste authentic Lowcountry cuisine. Reservations are accepted for dinner. Be sure to try their legendary

shrimp and grits. *Yum!* 207 Rutledge Avenue. http://hominygrill.com/

FYI: Charleston is all about history and food. It would take a reference the size of a phone book to include all food options in the greater Charleston area. One reason for all the dining options is that the Culinary Institute (Trident College) is in Charleston. Graduates don't have to go far to find great jobs. For a complete list of Charleston restaurants, check out https://charlestondining.com/.

3. See where the biggest event in America's history took place. From 1829 to 1845, 109,000 tons of rock and stone were used to create a 2.5-acre artificial island. Next, a pentagonal brick fort began to rise above the harbor's waters. **Fort Sumter** was designed to mount 135 guns and provide living space for 650 officers and soldiers. In December 1860, the fort was ninety percent complete, but construction stopped as soon as South Carolina passed the Ordinance of Secession. The first shots of the Civil War were fired from Fort Sumter on April 12, 1861. Although construction was never completed, the fort played a pivotal role throughout the war. When you're standing in the middle of the fort in the middle of August, you cannot

imagine that soldiers wore wool uniforms! This is a great experience for Civil War and nerdy history buffs—like me! https://www.nps.gov/fosu/index.htm

4. Take part in one of the best food festivals in the United States. The **Charleston Food and Wine Festival** is the place for foodies. Everyone who is anyone in the food industry has been a part of this annual

event. There are workshops, cooking demonstrations, signature dinners, wine tastings, and much more. Some celebrities have had trouble scoring tickets to some events, so be sure to book early. www.charlestonfoodandwine.com.

5. Pose for a picture in front of the iconic **Pineapple Fountain** in Waterfront Park. This twelve-acre, award-winning park is located along the Cooper River waterfront. It is a tourist rite of passage to have his or her photo taken with the fountain.

FYI: The pineapple is a symbol of hospitality and friendship, which is why you'll spot pineapple finials on posts and gates all over the city. Ship captains returning from the West Indies used to bring pineapples home to share with friends and family. Since we didn't have local pineapples, it was a cherished treat. Reportedly, captains would place a pineapple on his fence post to let everyone know he had safely returned from sea. It was also an invitation of sorts to stop in and catch up over refreshments.

6. Take a **Heavenly Charleston** church and graveyard walking tour. Charleston is known as the Holy City because it has the greatest concentration of churches in North America. Some date back to the 1600s. During this unique and uplifting 2.5-hour tour you will visit six historic churches, including some that are not open to any other tour group, and graveyards. The visit to the Unitarian Church cemetery alone is worth the tour. There is a twenty-person maximum for each tour, so be sure to book early. http://www.allaboutcharlestontours.com/heavenly-charleston

7. Another must is a **Gullah Tour**. You cannot truly experience Charleston without learning about Gullah folklore and history. During this two-hour bus tour led by Alphonso Brown (author of *A Gullah Guide to Charleston*), you

will visit Gullah historic sites, such as Catfish Row, Sweetgrass Market, and the African Methodist Church, while hearing remarkable stories and learning all about Gullah traditions, beliefs, and history. www.gullahtours.com.

8. **Charles Towne Landing State Historic Site** preserves the original site of the first permanent English settlement in Carolina. This 664-acre site provides a twenty-two acre natural habitat zoo, a museum, ongoing archeological excavations, miles of trails (bicycles permitted), tours, historic garden, cemetery, interpretive programs, a replica tall ship, six replica cannons, picnic area, the statue pictured here, and more. http://southcarolinaparks.com/ctl/introduction.aspx

FYI: About Charles Town Landing…

Statue at Charles Town Landing Historic Site

***It is the first permanent European settlement site in SC.**

***Six cannons that are fired on the 3rd Saturday of every month.**

******Adventure*** **is a replica of a 17th century trading ship that visitors can explore.**

***The zoo includes an Animal Forest, as well as bison and bears.**

***There are more than eighty acres of gardens and an alley of huge old oak trees.**

FYI: Three small ships carrying 148 English men and women sailed into the harbor in April 1670, and established the settlement of Charles Town, named in honor of King Charles II. Two settlers had died on the voyage, and many others were sick and malnourished upon arrival. Fortunately for the settlers, the ground was fertile and the Indians friendly, so the settlement survived and thrived. Within two years, the town was moved across the river to a peninsula, which was known as Oyster Point. Within five years, the town's population had quadrupled and Charles Town was a bustling seaport. The name was later changed to Charleston.

9. One of the best ways to experience this port city is on a boat, and it is especially lovely at night with all the lights of the city and the bridge lights. I highly recommend taking a **dinner sightseeing cruise**. Spirit Line Cruises offers a four-course dinner complete with live music and a full-service bar. Menus change but always include a fresh catch of the day, three or four entrees to choose from, soup, salad, and dessert. During this 2.5-hour cruise you will see the impressive Ravenel Bridge, as well as The Battery, Fort Sumter, the Charleston Harbor and waterfront, and enjoy a spectacular sunset. http://spiritlinecruises.com/dinner-cruises/.

10. I have to include the **Charleston Tea Plantation** because I am a tea drinker (admitted addict of hot tea and iced tea), so I make it a point to visit tea plantations when I travel. I have toured

them in Asia, South America, and Africa. The cool thing about the Charleston Tea Plantation is that it is the only tea plantation in North America. Plus, they have really beefed up their tours since I first visited, so it is worth the drive from Charleston to Wadmalaw Island. Nowadays, they offer year round educational tours of their factory and a video presentation, a trolley tour of the plantation (includes a stop at their greenhouse), and they have a large gift shop on site. Tea lovers should be sure to stock up on their famous Charleston Tea Plantation Peach Tea. http://www.charlestonteaplantation.com/.

I'm going to offer an alternative for those who have no interest in tea—or you can do both if time permits. The **Audubon Swamp Garden** is a unique world where trees grow from the water, islands float, and everywhere wild creatures go about their secret lives. It boasts a diversity of living things almost unequaled anywhere else in America Thousands of plant and animal species coexist amongst the cypress and tupelo gum trees, surrounded by blackwater. You can explore this wild and otherwise inaccessible landscape on boardwalks, bridges, and dikes. Be sure to look up and down to spot birds, reptiles, amphibians, and mammals, as well as flora and fauna. The Audubon Swamp Garden is part of Magnolia Plantation & Gardens, which is Charleston's most visited plantation. There is also an Audubon Swamp Tour, eco-tour by boat, nature train, petting zoo, peacocks, miniature horses, a maze, conservatory, orientation film, gift shop, and more. Open every day, year round. http://www.magnoliaplantation.com/swamp_garden.html

FYI: The Charleston Tea Plantation opened in 1987, but its origins date back to the 1700s when tea bushes first arrived in the United States from China. Several attempts were made over the next 150 years to propagate and produce tea for consumption, but none were successful.

Finally, in 1888, Dr. Charles Shepard founded the Pinehurst Tea Plantation in Summerville, SC and American grown tea became a reality. Dr. Shepard created award winning teas until his death in 1915.

After his death, the Pinehurst Tea Plantation closed, and Dr. Shepard's tea

plants grew wild for the next forty-five years.

In 1963, a 127-acre potato farm on Wadmalaw Island was bought, and Shepard's tea plants were transplanted from Summerville to Wadmalaw. This former potato farm eventually became known as the Charleston Tea Plantation. Every tea plant in Charleston Tea Plantation is a direct descendant of Dr. Shepard's 1888 crop!

South Carolina's soil and climate seems to be perfect for growing many kinds of crops.

TOURISTY THINGS TO SEE & DO

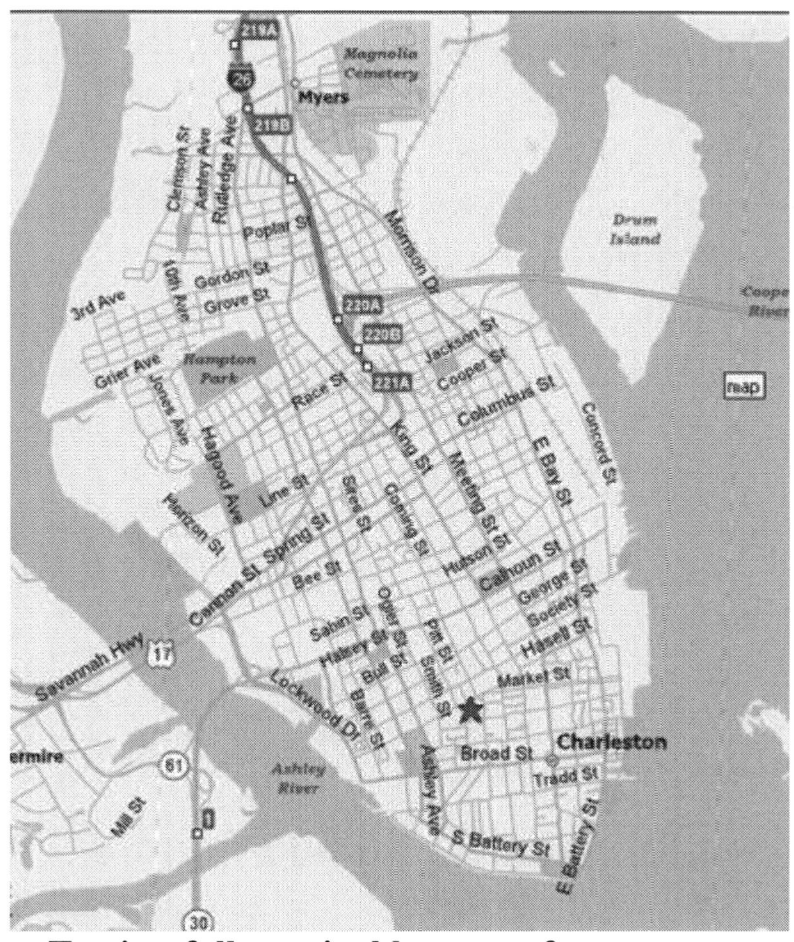

To view fully navigable maps of greater Charleston, http://www.things-to-do-in-charleston.com/charleston-maps.html

Aiken-Rhett House is a home built in 1820 at 48 Elizabeth Street in Charleston, South Carolina. It was a home of William Aiken, Jr., a governor of South Carolina, and before that was a home of his father, the railroad company owner William Aiken. http://www.charleston-sc.com/william-aiken-house.html

Audubon Swamp Garden is a 60-acre cypress and tupelo swamp on the grounds of Magnolia Plantation near Charleston, South Carolina. At one time, the swamp served as a reservoir for the plantation's rice cultivation. Today, the swamp garden includes native flora but also non-native, exotic plantings and is home to herons, ibis, turtles, otters, alligators, and other wildlife. http://www.magnoliaplantation.com/swamp_garden.html

The Battery (pictured here) is a seawall and promenade in downtown Charleston. Named for a Civil War defense artillery battery at the site, The Battery is a park, and it is also where some of the finest homes in Charleston are located.

FYI: Turkey Buzzards, dubbed "Charleston Eagles," were once used to keep the streets clean outside the city's marketplace. This helped prevent the spread of disease and kept the city looking nice.

Charleston's iconic Broad Street

Boone Hall Plantation is one of America's oldest working plantations, continually growing crops for over 320 years. The antebellum era plantation is located in Mount Pleasant, Charleston County, South Carolina, U.S.A., and listed on the National Register of Historic Places. www.boonehallplantation.com

Calhoun Mansion is a Victorian house at 16 Meeting St., Charleston, South Carolina. The mansion is open for public tours. It was built for George W. Williams, a businessman, according to plans drawn by W.P. Russell. http://www.calhounmansion.net/

Cannon Park is a 2.7-acre public park that is bounded to the north by Calhoun Street and to the south by Bennett Street. To the east is Rutledge Avenue and to the west is Ashley Avenue.

Colonial Lake

Capers Island is a state-owned barrier island roughly fifteen miles north of Charleston. There is lots of wildlife, birding, fishing and the eerily beautiful Boneyard Beach. Nature tours are offered by http://nature-tours.com/capers-island/

Charleston Museum is one of the oldest museums in the United States. It's highly regarded collection includes ancient artifacts, natural history displays, decorative arts, and two historic houses. www.charlestonmuseum.org

Charles Towne Landing State Historic Site preserves the original site of the first permanent English settlement in Carolina. This 664-acre site is home to an exhibit hall, rental facility, a natural habitat zoo, ongoing archeological excavations, miles of trails, a large picnic area, a replica tall ship, six cannons, and much more. http://southcarolinaparks.com/ctl/introduction.aspx

Children's Museum of the Lowcountry has numerous exhibits, a pirate ship, art room, and two-story medieval castle. www.exploreCML.org

City Market is a historic market area in downtown Charleston. Established in the 1790s, this market complex stretches for four city blocks. It starts at Market Hall, which has been described as a building of the "highest architectural design quality." http://www.thecharlestoncitymarket.com/

Confederate Museum is operated by the United Daughters of the Confederacy, Charleston Chapter 4. It features memorabilia from the American Civil War. www.theconfederatemuseum.com

Daniel Island is a 4,000-acre island located within Charleston's city limits and situated between the Cooper and Wando Rivers. Daniel Island is a master-planned community complete with residential neighborhoods, parks, trails, shops, restaurants, schools, churches, and other businesses. www.danielisland.org

Drayton Hall is an 18th-century plantation located on the Ashley River about fifteen miles northwest of Charleston. It is the only plantation house on the Ashley River to survive intact throughout both the Revolutionary and Civil Wars. It is a National Historic Landmark. www.draytonhall.org

Dock Street Theatre opened on February 12, 1736, with a performance of *The Recruiting Officer*. It was the first building in America built exclusively for theatrical performances. A fire destroyed it, and a hotel was built in its place. Eventually, the hotel was converted into a theatre and it once again became the Dock Street Theatre. A $20 million renovation was completed in 2010. Dock Street is one of the most haunted places in Charleston and is on the National Register of Historic Places in 1973. https://www.charlestonstage.com/dock-street-theatre.html

Folly Beach is a city on a nineteen-mile barrier island, Folly Island. Iconic The Folly Island

Fishing Pier (Pictured here) stretches more than 1,000-feet into the Atlantic. www.follybeach.com

Fort Sumter is a sea fort where two Civil War battles were fought, including the first shot of the war. Tour boats to Fort Sumter are provided by Fort Sumter Tours, the authorized concessioner of Fort Sumter National Monument. Departures are at Liberty Square and Patriots Point. The National Park Service highly recommends purchasing tickets in advance. For more information, www.FortSumterTours.com

Gibbes Museum of Art houses a premier collection of over 10,000 works of fine art, many with a connection to Charleston or the South. www.gibbesmuseum.org

Heyward-Washington House was built in 1772. It was home to Thomas Heyward, Jr., a signer of the United States Declaration of Independence, and it was where George Washington stayed during his visit to the city. Furnished for the late 18th century, the house includes a collection of Charleston-made furniture. In addition to the house museum, there is a carriage house and 1740s kitchen outbuilding. http://www.charlestonmuseum.org/historic-houses/heyward-washington-house/

H. L. Hunley was a submarine of the Confederate States of America that played a role in the Civil War. She was the first submarine to sink a warship, but sadly the ship and twenty-one-member crew were lost as a result of this encounter. The sub has been excavated, and tours are offered to view the ongoing preservation process. www.hunley.org

Joseph Manigault House was built in 1803 and serves as a fine example of Adam-style architecture. http://www.charlestonmuseum.org/historic-houses/joseph-manigault-house/

Isle of Palms is a city and a barrier island. The town lies along a narrow strip of land, separated from the mainland by the Intracoastal Waterway. There are large beachfront homes, resorts, and some local businesses. www.iop.net

Kiawah is an island that lies twenty-five miles southwest of Charleston. Kiawah Island Golf Resort comprises most of the island with spacious villas, pools, restaurants, tennis courts, championship golf courses, and The Sanctuary Hotel Resort. www.kiawahisland.org

Aerial view of Charleston Peninsula with Arthur J. Ravenel Bridge in background

Magnolia Cemetery, dedicated in 1850, is on the land of a former rice plantation. This cemetery is considered to be one of the best examples of rural and Victorian cemetery design in America. Many famous folks are buried here. It is a lovely place with lots of green space, trees, landscaped paths, and ponds. This cemetery is listed on the National Register of Historic Places. www.magnoliacemetery.net

Magnolia Plantation and Gardens overlooks the Ashley River. It is one of the oldest plantations in the South. The house and gardens are open daily; an admission fee is charged. www.magnoliaplantation.com

Marion Square spans more than six acres in downtown Charleston. It is named in honor of Francis Marion.

McLeod Plantation Historic Site dates back to 1851.This thirty-seven-acre Gullah/Geechee heritage site has been preserved in recognition of its cultural and historical significance. The grounds include a riverside outdoor pavilion, a sweeping oak alley, and the McLeod Oak, which is thought to be more than 600 years old. The admission fee includes a 45-minute interpretive tour. http://ccprc.com/1447/McLeod-Plantation-Historic-Site

Middleton Place is a plantation located fifteen miles northwest of Charleston, in the Built in several phases during the 18th and 19th centuries, the plantation was the primary residence of several generations of the Middleton family, many of whom played prominent roles in the colonial and antebellum history of South Carolina. Today, it is a museum and home to the oldest landscaped gardens in the United States. www.middletonplace.org

Morris Island Lighthouse (pictured here) stands on the southern side of the Charleston Harbor on Morris Island, which is north of Folly Beach. The lighthouse, built in 1876, has been on the National Register of Historic Places since 1982. You can't go into or even out to the lighthouse, but you can get a good view of it from the beach and on some harbor cruises. 2223 Folly Road. www.savethelight.org

Music Farm is arguably the best music venue in the greater Charleston area. Owner Kevin Wadley wanted a venue that focused on music, not just another nightclub. Wadley originated the name and concept for Music Farm. It has gained a reputation nightspot throughout the Southeast as "the place" to hear good music. www.musicfarm.org

Nathaniel Russell House was built by wealthy shipping merchant Nathaniel Russell in 1808. It is recognized as one of America's most important neoclassical houses. https://www.historiccharleston.org/Russell.aspx

Old Exchange & Provost Dungeon was built in 1767-71 and has served as a Customs House, prisoner of war facility during the American Revolutionary War, and a museum. This is one of the most historically significant buildings in the city and is also reportedly haunted. www.oldexchange.org

Postal Museum chronicle's Charleston's postal history. It is inside the old post office at the corner of Meeting and Broad Streets.

Powder Magazine is the oldest surviving public building in South Carolina. It was used as a gunpowder store through the American Revolutionary War and later saw other uses. It has been operated as a museum by the National Society of the Colonial Dames of America since the early 1900s. www.powdermagazine.org

Rainbow Row

Rainbow Row is the name for a row of thirteen historic houses in Charleston that seem to be painted every color in the rainbow. It represents the longest cluster of Georgian row houses in the United States. The houses are located north of Tradd St. and south of Elliott St. on East Bay

Street—from 79 to 107 East Bay Street. It is a popular tourist attraction and is one of the most photographed parts of Charleston.

Seabrook Island is a private, barrier island. Only homeowners and guests with dinner reservations at Sea Island Club are permitted on the island. www.discoverseabrook.com

South Carolina Aquarium is home to more than ten thousand plants and animals including North American river otters, loggerhead sea turtles, alligators, great blue herons, owls, seahorses, pufferfish, green moray eels, sharks, and more. The largest exhibit is the Great Ocean Tank, which extends from the first to the third floor of the Aquarium and contains more than seven hundred animals. The Aquarium also features a Touch Tank, where patrons may touch stingrays and other marine animals. www.scaquarium.org

Old Slave Mart Museum was once used the site of slave auctions. Once part of a complex of buildings, the Slave Mart is the only structure to remain. It is believed to be the last extant slave auction facility in South Carolina. Around 1878, the Slave Mart was renovated into a two-story tenement dwelling. In 1938, the property was purchased by Miriam B. Wilson, who turned the site into a museum of African American history, arts and crafts. It is one of many buildings in Charleston that is on the National Register of Historic Places. 6 Chalmers Street. http://www.oldslavemartmuseum.com/

Patriots Point (pictured here) is a naval and maritime museum. A general admission ticket gets you access to all exhibits, including *USS Yorktown, USS Laffey, USS Clamagore*, The Vietnam Experience Exhibit, Cold War Memorial, and the Medal of Honor Museum. Patriots Point also offers a flight academy and slumber parties! Campers sleep in the berths that sailors once occupied. Packages include lodging, meals, and educational activities. www.patriotspoint.org

Sullivan's Island at the entrance to Charleston Harbor. The town dates back to 1817, known at that time as Moultrieville. There are no hotels, motels, inns, or lodging on the island except for vacation home rentals. There are some historic attractions on the island, including Fort Moultrie and Sullivan's Island Lighthouse, which is one of the last beacons to be built in America. http://sullivansisland-sc.com/

Washington Square Park is a lovely park in the center of Charleston that is full of azaleas and live oaks dripping with Spanish moss.

Waterfront Park is easily recognized by its Pineapple Fountain.

Waterfront Park is a twelve-acre park along overlooking the Cooper River.

West Ashley is one of the six distinct areas west of the Ashley River. There are dozens of neighborhoods and shopping areas, including The Citadel Mall.

White Point Garden is a 5.7-acre public park bounded by East Battery, Murray Boulevard, King Street, and South Battery.

***Be warned!* Gators, like hurricanes, humidity, and shrimp & grits, are part of the South Carolina Lowcountry. You'll find them on golf courses, under boardwalks, in marshes and ponds, and underneath porches. Here is a sign warning visitors at the Audubon Swamp.**

Typically, they don't bother you if you don't bother them, but it is best to keep a close eye on children and pets.

FYI: ***And the award for the most unique museum goes to*****…North Charleston FIRE MUSEUM, which has many exhibits, collections, and activities. This includes twenty fire trucks dating back to 1785! www.northcharlestonfiremuseum.org**

Charleston Tours

Bulldog Tours offers good history, ghost, and food tours. In fact, they offer several intriguing ghost tours, including a paranormal investigation of one of the most haunted places in Charleston. https://bulldogtours.com/. Other sightseeing tours include https://www.adventuresightseeing.com/tours.cf

m#.WLH2RoWcGUk
https://charleston.com/gray-line-of-charleston

Carolina Queen is a paddlewheel riverboat that offers some great theme cruises, such as a murder mystery cruise, jazz brunch cruises, and Blues & BBQ cruises. www.charlestonharbortours.com

Carriage Ride & Sightseeing Tour are popular with tourists. In fact, some believe that no visit to Charleston is complete without a horse-drawn

carriage ride. Public and private tours are offered. www.palmettocarriage.com, https://www.oldsouthcarriagetours.com/, and https://cpcc.com/

Charleston Chef's Kitchen Walking Culinary Tour is a guided walking culinary tour that lasts 2.5 hours, but only covers six blocks or so. You will leisurely tour the kitchens and sample pastries, biscuits and other traditional southern dishes from five different eateries. https://charlestonculinarytours.com/

Charleston Pirate Tour is good for all ages. See the city's highlights and learn all about its dark history, including the Golden Age of Piracy. You will explore, learn, and have fun! https://www.charlestonpiratetour.com/

Charleston Tavern Tour is for those interested in learning more about Charleston's pubs, pirates, patriots, police, priests, and prostitutes.

You will hear strange but true stories while exploring area taverns and partaking in a sip or two of local brews. www.charlestonpiratetour.com

Gullah Tour is a two-hour, reservations required tour that departs from the Charleston Visitor's Center. It is conducted on a twenty-one passenger, air conditioned bus, so participants are comfortable any time of year. In addition to seeing Gullah historic sites, stories are shared about Gullah traditions, language, and culture. http://gullahtours.com/

Harbor Cruises shows you 75 points of interest from a two-deck (inside climate-controlled or outside Observation Deck). Harbor Cruises can be combined with carriage tours or plantation tours. https://www.charlestonharbortours.com/ and http://spiritlinecruises.com/charleston-harbor-tours/

Haunted Harbor Ghost & Pirate Tour is the only ghost and pirate tour offered on the water in

Charleston. Tours depart from the Charleston Maritime Center. http://www.sandlappertours.com/ghost-tours/

Helicopter Tours are affordable aerial sightseeing tours. Get a bird's eye view of Charleston! www.flyinhelicopters.com

Jewish Tours (Chai Y'All Tours) are led by the founder of the SC Jewish Historical Society. These tours have been featured in Southern Living as a "Top 5 City Tour." http://discoversouthcarolina.com/products/25651

Lowcountry Loop Trolley is a hop on, hop off service to Mt. Pleasant, Sullivan's Island, Isle of Palms, and Charleston. They also offer tours to Firefly Distillery, Charleston Tea Plantation, and Boone Hall. www.looptrolley.com

Pub & Brewery Tours of Charleston features the Original Pub Tour, Upper King Street Pub Crawl, and a Brewery Bus Tour. http://pubtourcharleston.com/

Sailing Tour aboard the *Schooner Pride* offers non-narrated daily sailing excursions or romantic sunset sails that promise participants escape the crowded streets and sweltering heat of downtown Charleston, SC. Enjoy a serene harbor two-hour tour complete with the peaceful waters of Charleston Harbor, as we mingle with dolphins, pelicans, and seagulls. https://www.schoonerpride.com/

Sandlapper Water Tours offer a choice of History, Nature, Dinner, or Sunset Cruises that are led by local historians and naturalists aboard a 45-foot catamaran. www.sandlappertours.com

Sites and Insights Tours (Black History, Porgy & Bess, and Sea Islands Tours) explores Charleston's black history and the Gullah, which includes Charleston and area sea islands. www.sitesandinsightstours.com

***USS Yorktown* Aircraft Carrier Ghost Tours** combine adventure with paranormal. The

legendary WWII aircraft carrier, *USS Yorktown*, is surrounded by mystery and intrigue. Just six days after construction began on the vessel, the Japanese attacked Pearl Harbor. During her commissioned duty she earned eleven battle stars. Many paranormal events reportedly take place aboard this ship, known by many as the Fighting Lady. More than 100 crew members lost their lives while serving aboard this ship, which may help explain the paranormal activity. Learn about strange activity reported over the years, like shadowy figures, footsteps echoing through the corridors and mysterious voices. Find out the results of an investigation of the vessel by Syfy Channel's Ghost Hunters. This interesting guided tour will take you through a haunted history, including tales of war heroes, lives lost, and ghosts which some believe haunt the ship. You'll be equipped with a ghost meter so that you can do your own detecting during this 90-minute tour.
https://yorktownghosttours.com/

Since Charleston is one of the most haunted cities in America, there are lots of ghost walks and graveyard tours, including www.bulldogtours.com, www.charlestonghostsofthesouth.com, www.ghostwalk.net, www.walksofcharleston.com, and www.oldcharlestontours.com. One of the most haunted places in Charleston is the Old City Jail. Bulldog Tours offers a Haunted Jail Tour that some say is the scariest experience they've ever had. Past participants say they have seen objects move or even disappear, They have also heard disembodied voices, doors slamming, and chains rattling. However, I prefer their Haunted Dungeon Tour.

Here is a list of historic churches in downtown Charleston:

Bethel Methodist Church, 222 Calhoun Street

Cathedral of St. John the Baptist, 120 Broad Street

Cathedral of St. Luke and St. Paul, 126 Coming Street

Central Baptist Church, 26 Radcliffe Street

Circular Congregational Church, 150 Meeting Street

Emanuel A.M.E. Church, 110 Calhoun Street

First Baptist Church, 61 Church Street

First Scots Presbyterian Church, 53 Meeting Street

French Huguenot Church, 44 Queen Street

Grace Episcopal Church, 98 Wentworth Street

Kahal Kadosh Beth Elohim, 90 Hasell Street

St. Johns Lutheran Church, 5 Clifford Street

St. Luke's Chapel, 181 Ashley Avenue

St. Mary's Catholic Church, 89 Hasell Street

St. Matthews Lutheran Church, 405 King Street

St. Michaels Episcopal Church, 71 Broad Street

St. Philip's Church, 142 Church Street

Unitarian Church in Charleston, 8 Archdale Street

Activities

Hike, paddleboard, kayak, and canoe with **Nature Adventures**. They offer adventure camps, eco-tours, and overnight adventure trips. http://www.kayakcharlestonsc.com/index.php

Go zip lining. www.charlestonziplineadventures.com is the only zip line canopy tour in the Charleston area, and they offer zip lining for younger children (ages 5 -10).

For a list of golf and tennis clubs, https://charleston.com/visiting-charleston/things-to-do/golf-tennis

Explore Charleston's backroads by bike with **Charleston Bicycle Tours**. Several different options are available including multi-day bike tours. www.charlestonbicycletours.com

Go Flyboarding. A jet ski generates the power, and a 50-foot hose redirects the water from the ski to the Flyboard. The rider hovers in the air for as long they want. Hydroflynow also offers wakeboarding and tubing.
http://www.hydroflynow.com/

FYI: There are numerous activities to do in greater Charleston, including dinner cruises,

fishing, kayaking, parasailing, dolphin encounters, jet skiing, scuba diving, party cruises, and more. Furthermore, there are many annual events and attractions in North Charleston, Mount Pleasant, Shem Creek, Isle of Palms, Sullivan's Island, Folly Beach, Kiawah Island, and Seabrook Island. Resources for these activities include www.aqua-safaris.com, www.charlestonoutdooradventures.com, www.coastalexpeditions.com, and www.kayakcharlestonsc.com.

Also, Charleston has three sports teams, Charleston Riverdogs (baseball), South Carolina Stingrays (hockey), and Charleston Battery Soccer. For a list of theatres and performing arts centers, http://www.charlestoncvb.com/plan-your-trip/arts-culture-entertainment~206/theater-theater-venues~1174/. For more tourism information visit http://www.charlestoncvb.com/beaches/.

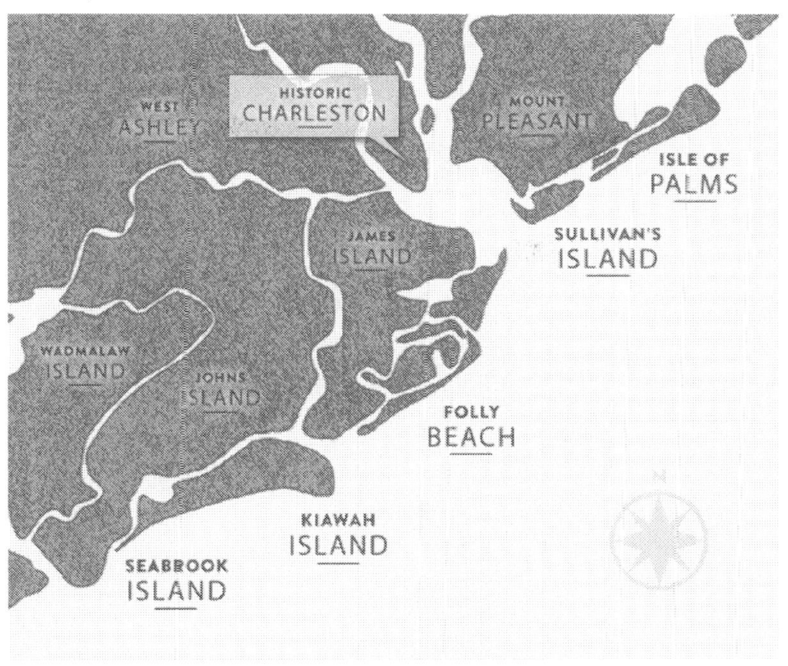

From Charleston to…

Mount Pleasant=5 miles

James Island=6 miles

Sullivan's Island=9 miles

Folly Beach=11 miles

Isle of Palms=13 miles

John's Island=13 miles

Wadmalaw Island=19 miles

Seabrook=25 miles

Kiawah=30 miles

BEST OF CHARLESTON

Tours, attractions, historic sites, and activities are addressed in the TOURISTY THINGS TO DO chapter. For more tourism information, visit www.charlestoncvb.com.

BEST PLACES FOR SOUVENIRS:

Magnifilous Toy Emporium is the best place for kids. 525 King Street. http://www.magnifilous.com/

The Shops at Charleston Place has lots of elite stores, such as Chico's, Gucci, Godiva, and

Tommy Bahama. 205 Meeting Street. http://www.belmond.com/charleston-place/shopping_charleston

Charleston City Market is the place to go to find Lowcountry souvenirs, including Charleston Tea Plantation products, Gullah Sweetgrass Baskets, tins of Benne Wafers, and more. They are open during the day and evenings too on Fridays and Saturdays. 188 Meeting. Street. http://www.thecharlestoncitymarket.com/

King Street is unofficially divided into three shopping areas: Upper King Street (design stores), Middle King Street (fashion shops), and Lower King Street (antiques, art galleries, and gift stores). https://www.charlestonsfinest.com/sc/exclusking.htm

Citadel Mall, one of the largest shopping malls in the state, is a 1,138,527 square feet shopping mall featuring more than 100 stores, including six anchor stores. www.citadelmall.net

FYI: Chattanooga Bakery produced over 100 items but they knew they had something special with MoonPie®. At 5¢ each, Moon Pies were an affordable, filling snack that just flew off the shelves. By 1929, the factory ladies were boxing up hundreds every day. When our brave servicemen went to war, Moon Pies went with them. Nothing said home more than a care-package filled with their favorite hometown snack. From the frontlines to the home front, MoonPie was the comfort food the nation turned to during the heroic days of World War II. You can't believe how many flavors there are! 48 North Market Street.

BEST PLACE TO STAY: Overlooking Marion Square, the **Francis Marion Hotel** is one of Charleston's finest. Offering guest rooms, suites, and penthouse suites, this hotel has every amenity a guest could want, including a spa, award-winning restaurant, conference facilities, and piano bar. http://francismarionhotel.com/. More about lodging can be found in the ABOUT ACCOMMODATIONS chapter.

BEST LIVE MUSIC: Pour House hosts all kinds of musicians. It is hard to beat their back deck, beer, and shows. They offer both free and paid shows. 1977 Maybank Highway. http://charlestonpourhouse.com/

BEST BOOKSTORE: Blue Bicycle Books is an independent bookstore that was established in 1995. They have new and used books—and lots of them too! They host more than 200 author events annually. 420 Meeting Street. http://bluebicyclebooks.com/the-store/.

BEST SPA: The Sanctuary Spa on Kiawah Island. I have super sensitive skin, so spa treatments are usually a no-no for me. No matter what I'm told about how wonderful their hypoallergenic products and treatments are, it never ends well. But this spa is wonderful. I have never had a problem with anything they've used on my face and always leave feeling "reborn." Be warned that it is not cheap so be prepared to spend some money if you want to pamper yourself. www.kiawahresort.com/spa

BEST ROOFTOP BAR: Rooftop Bar at Vendue is the place for cool cocktails, great view, and lunch or dinner. They often feature live music. http://www.thevendue.com/dining/the-rooftop/#5NX4JP. Runner Up: **Eleve** in the Grand Bohemian Hotel.

BEST SOUTHERN CUISINE RESTAURANT: Husk is the place to try the regional cuisine. If you don't believe me, just listen to their motto, "If it doesn't come from the South, it's not coming through the door," says Chef Brock. 76 Queen Street. www.huskrestaurant.com.

BEST LOWCOUNTRY CUISINE: 82 Queen serves brunch, lunch, and dinner. Reservations suggested for dinner. 82 Queen Street. www.82queen.com.

BEST CHARLESTON ICON: Red's Icehouse on Shem Creek has been around since 1947. Red has been gone from this world since the 1990s, but his tradition of serving fresh, local seafood in a casual, comfortable place lives on. **Runner UP:** Since 1890, **Hyman's Seafood** has been satisfying customers with fresh seafood and good times. www.hymanseafood.com http://www.redsicehouse.com/

BEST FINE DINING: Circa 1886 holds a Forbes Four Star distinction, AAA Four Diamond rating and has been recognized by Wine Enthusiast as one of America's Best Wine Restaurants. They feature a seasonal menu using local ingredients. It is inside the former carriage house for the Wentworth Mansion. 149 Wentworth Street. https://www.circa1886.com/restaurant/overview/

BEST CHAMPAGNE BAR: For those looking for a special spot, tucked away in a corner of the Peninsula Grill is the **Peninsula Grill Champagne Bar**. It features signature cocktails and specialty drinks. 112 N. Market Street. https://www.peninsulagrill.com/main/restaurant-champagne-bar

BEST VIEW: *See* **BEST ROOFTOP BAR.**

BEST GOLF COURSE: Kiawah Island Golf Resort's The Ocean Course is one of only four courses in the U.S. to have hosted every major PGA event in the U.S. and is ranked in the Top 100 Golf Courses by *Golf Digest*. But they also have four more championship courses in case you get tired of this one—that's 90 holes! Plus, the resort has ten miles of beach, three pool complexes, an award-winning spa, and tennis. www.kiawahresort.com

BEST PLACE FOR JAZZ MUSIC: Charleston Grill is the place to go to hear great jazz. 224 King Street. http://www.charlestongrill.com/web/ochg/charleston_jazz.jsp

BEST FAMILY RESTAURANT: Five Loaves Café works with local farms to provide fresh vegetables and vegetarian options, serves antibiotic-free chicken raised in the Carolinas, they only serve hormone-free and pasture-raised beef. They have a good kids menu, and all of their selections are $1-$6. They have great daily specials and serve Sunday brunch. 43 Cannon Street. www.fiveloavescafe.com

BEST OYSTER BAR: The Ordinary is a seafood hall and oyster ball located in an old bank at 544 King Street. They feature SC Littleneck Clams, SC Peel & Eat Shrimp, and East Coast Oysters. If you like oysters, you have to try their Crispy Fried Oyster Sliders. They offer daily specials, including Baked Stuffed Lobster (yum!) on Fridays. http://eattheordinary.com/

BEST CLASSIC CHARLESTON RESTAURANT: Poogan's Porch is my favorite restaurant. This award-winning eatery has delicious food, a nice ambiance (It is an adorable Victorian house), and a ghost or two! Furthermore, they boast a 1,500-bottle wine cellar. And you can't beat their brunch. I highly recommend the Lowcountry Omelet and Pimento BLT. 72 Queen Street. www.poogansporch.com.

BEST BAGELS: Blondies Bagels & Café not only features a dozen homemade bagels but also many flavors of homemade cream cheese. http://www.blondiesdi.com/

BEST ASIAN & SUSHI: Zen's Asian Fusion offers everything from soups to entrees, including Coconut Shrimp, Tom Yam Seafood Hot and Sour Soup, Summer Rolls, and Pad Thai. http://www.zenasianrestaurant.com/index.html

BEST PIZZA: Andolini's makes their dough, grates their cheese, and makes fresh sauce daily. http://andolinis.com/

BEST CUPCAKES: Cupcakes Down South offers more than fifty varieties of cupcakes, including white chocolate strawberry champagne, lemon squeeze (yummy!), and loco for coco. They have vegan and gluten-free cupcakes too. http://freshcupcakes.com/

BEST PLACE FOR DESSERT: Gala Desserts. You name it; they got it! In addition to every kind of dessert you can think of (they even serve mini desserts for those watching their weight), they serve espresso, lattes, juice, coffee, tea, beer, wine, tapas, Paninis (try the chicken), breakfast, and more. And the prices are reasonable too! 829 Savannah Highway. https://www.galadesserts.com/

BEST DESSERT TOUR: During this two-hour Charleston Dessert Tour offered by Bulldog Tours, you will sample six of the Lowcountry's best desserts, including Southern Pralines and Huguenot Tort. *Yum!* https://bulldogtours.com/charleston-dessert-tour/

BEST ROWDY BAR: Royal American is probably is eclectic and rowdy as Charleston gets. If you want rowdy, you got to head to a beach bar. To give you an idea of what it's like, Christmas lights and old National Geographic magazines serve as decorations. Their signature shot is the Royal American Cinnamon Whiskey. The often have live music and serve Frito Pie, as well as homemade beef jerky. Now you got to go just to see this place, right? 970 Morrison Avenue. www.theroyalamerican.com

BEST SPORTS BAR: *Literally!* This retro bowling alley, aptly named **The Alley**, offers bowling seven days a week and serves pub food and craft beer. They also have an arcade and lots of big screen TVs displaying every major college and pro ball games. 131 Columbus Street. www.thealleycharleston.com.

BEST COMBINATION: Fish is a restaurant by day and doubles as a nightclub, Club Fish, come late night. It is the hotspot of choice for young, professional Charlestonians. There is a DJ and dancing and a line if you don't come early. 442 King Street.

BEST HIPSTER BAR: Closed for Business is the hippest place to have a beer with close to fifty beers on tap. 453 King Street. www.closed4business.com.

Runner Up: The Gin Joint at 182 E. Bay Street. www.theginjoint.com.

BEST ALTERNATIVE BAR: Cure Nightclub is renowned for their drag shows and arguably the best music in town. 28 Ann Street. www.curenightclub.com.

FYI: There are so many bars and nightclubs in Charleston that I recommend you check out TripAdvisor to see reviews and learn more about which ones appeal to you. The beauty of Charleston is there is something for everyone, and there are more places than you can ever visit if you include all the places in the greater Charleston area, such as Folly Beach, Sullivan's Island, and Mount Pleasant.

Main Streets in Charleston, SC

Legare Street is pronounced "luh-gree." It is named in honor of an 18th-century merchant, and has some of the most magnificent houses, gates, and gardens in the city, not to mention lovely magnolias and live oaks. Only four blocks long, Legare Street is famous for Sword Gate and Pineapple Gatehouse.

Broad Street was originally known as Cooper Street. It was later changed to Broad to reflect that it is the widest of the city's original passageways. In addition to area businesses, Broad Street also boasts some historic residences, including houses owned by John and Edward Rutledge, signers of the Constitution and Declaration. The "Four Corners of Law" includes Broad Street and the Old Exchange can be found on this street.

Tradd Street is named for the first family to have a child in the new colony. Tradd Street is remarkably unchanged from the earliest days of Charleston and boasts more 18th century houses than most cities in America. To the west, you can see the Ashley River, and to the east, the Cooper River can be seen.

King Street is known as the shopping district. *Ladies, this is where you go to shop 'til you drop!* Upper King is known as the Design District, Middle King is the Fashion District, and Lower King is the Antique District. Lower King also has many art galleries and gift shops.

East Battery Street is one of the shortest in the city, but perhaps the best known. It extends from the point of the peninsula to Water Street, where it becomes East Bay Street. Many original houses still stand, including the Roper House, which features lion's head earthquake plates and still holds a piece of Civil War cannon barrel in its attic, from an explosion during a Civil War skirmish in 1865 that sent part of the cannon into the house.

Church Street is named for all its churches, including St. Philip's Episcopal Church. Church Street winds through South of Broad, which is lined with elegant houses and grand gardens. The street terminates at the famous White Point Gardens at the tip of the old peninsula.

FYI: Charleston's Downtown is also known as The Peninsula. It is a 4.5-mile area, which is less than eight feet above sea level and on occasion is actually slightly below sea level.

Pink House, constructed of pinkish Bermuda stone, was built 1694 – 1712. Its original purpose was a tavern, but it is now an art gallery and local icon. 17 Chalmers Street.

ABOUT ACCOMMODATIONS

Accommodations vary greatly in Charleston, but most places in downtown Charleston are not for the budget-minded. Charleston has many fine hotels and inns, such as The Elliot House, French Quarter Inn, Andrew Pinckney Inn, HarbourView Inn, King Charles Inn, Fulton Lane Inn, Planters Inn, Battery Carriage House Inn, John Rutledge House Inn, Kings Courtyard Inn, The Wentworth Mansion, and Restoration on King.

Another option is to stay in nearby places, such as Sullivan's Island, Mount Pleasant, and North Charleston. You can stay in a small B & B or a large resort. You can stay in a boutique hotel or rental property. The best deals will be on vacation rentals or specials found through sites like www.AirBnB.com, www.Priceline.com, www.Trivago.com, www.Hotels.com, or www.Booking.com. You can also check out www.thecottagesoncharlestonharbor.com, www.dunesproperties.com, www.WVRCharleston.com, and www.beachwalker.com,

If you are on a budget, you will have to use one of the sites above to book a rental or stay outside of downtown Charleston. Also, look for seasonal specials and discounted packages on resort websites. AAA, AARP, military and government employees receive discounted rates at most places. You should be able to negotiate a better rate than what you see advertised by calling the property directly, especially if it is not peak season. Rates are highest at Christmas, Easter and for special annual events.

BEST CAMPING

Campground at James Island County Park Charleston County Park & Recreation Commission (options include camping (http://www.ccprc.com/1434/Campground), cottages (http://www.ccprc.com/1435/The-Cottages), and the lovely Lake House at Bulow, http://www.ccprc.com/1519/The-Lake-House-at-Bulow
and http://www.ccprc.com/1729/Camping-Lodging

Runner Ups:
Charleston Kampgrounds of America offers cabins, camping, and more.
9494 Hwy 78, Ladson, SC

Fain's RV Park is a favorite of the men and women at Charleston Air Force Base. It is near many local attractions and has plenty of amenities. I-26 Exit 211A, 6309 Fain Blvd., Charleston, SC 29418

KOA of Mt. Pleasant is on the grounds of an old 377-acre plantation, Oakland Plantation. They offer lots of extras too, such as free weekend hayrides and lakefront Kamping Kabooses. Blackbeard's Cove Family Fun Park is next door. 3157 N. Hwy 17, Mt. Pleasant, SC 29464

Lake Aire RV Park & Campground is just minutes from downtown Charleston. Located on thirty-two acres, this campground offers 87 RV sites and 26 campsites. 4375 Highway 172, Hollywood, SC 29449

Oak Plantation Campground boasts 250 campsites, a swimming pool, store, and more. 3540 Savannah Hwy, Charleston, SC 29407

<u>BEST HOSTEL</u>

Charleston NotSo Hostel is located in an enclave of double-porched houses from the 1840's conveniently located in the downtown historic district of Charleston, SC. They offer both dorm rooms and private rooms and have four kitchens and bathrooms that are shared among guests. There are lockers, safe deposit boxes, and vending machines. There is free parking, free city maps, free breakfast, free Wi-Fi, free linens, and free laundry facilities. Bike rentals are available. www.notsohostel.com

BEST BOUTIQUE HOTEL

Jasmine House Inn is a beautifully renovated mansion dating back to 1843. It combines the charm of a B&B and the comfort of a luxury hotel. It is cozy with only twelve rooms, but they are large and luxurious with hardwood floors, high ceilings, big TVs, and tasteful furnishings and décor. They provide free breakfast, free Wi-Fi, and free evening hors d'oeuvres. www.jasminehouseinn.com

BEST LUXURY HOTEL

Market Pavilion Hotel is a luxurious property located in the heart of the Historic District. From Hermes toiletries to their Concierge Level, they've thought of everything. There is a great rooftop bar, fine steakhouse, and lovely pool. www.marketpavilion.com

BEST BARGAIN BEACH HOTEL

The Tides Folly Beach is a newly remodeled waterfront property with 132 rooms. Balconied rooms overlook the outdoor heated pool and ocean. They have quite a few amenities, including Starbucks coffee, outdoor bar, and lounge, oceanfront restaurant, room service, free parking, pets allowed, business center. And they have some great packages, including their Folly Beach Mystery Package, based on author Bill Noel's mystery series. www.tidesfollybeach.com

BEST LUXURY BEACH RESORT

The Sanctuary on Kiawah Island. If you have deep pockets, this is THE place to stay. I'm talking right a five-star resort right on the beach, an award-winning spa, the best shops, indoor and outdoor pools, fine dining, championship golf, and more. You will not find better service anywhere—there's even a beach concierge! www.thesanctuary.com

BEST HIPSTER HOTEL

Grand Bohemian Hotel offers 50 luxury rooms, Grand Bohemian Gallery, a rooftop terrace, wine blending room, crafted cocktails, and more. www.grandbohemiancharleston.com

BEST FAMILY-FRIENDLY HOTEL

Hampton Inn Charleston Historic District, housed in a former railroad warehouse, has 171 rooms that are clean, cozy, and comfortable, featuring mahogany furniture. Located on the edge of the Historic Downtown, it is within walking distance, and there is free trolley service. There's also an outdoor pool and more family-oriented amenities. http://hamptoninn3.hilton.com/en/hotels/south-carolina/hampton-inn-charleston-historic-district-CHSHDHX/index.html

BEST HOTEL RESTAURANT

At Zero George, *"Urbane and Welcoming Tradition meets Southern Chic."* Circa 1804, the sixteen studios and suites are located in a landscaped enclave surrounded by three Charleston residences and two brick carriage houses. All guestrooms feature original architectural elements including heart pine floors, high ceilings, period millwork details and classic piazzas. Their restaurant has earned the "Top Five

Foodie Hotel in the World Award." http://zerogeorge.com/

BEST ADULTS ONLY

La Mer Hotel & Dewey House is right on the beach. Bottled water, breakfast, turndown service, private balcony, and afternoon refreshments are included. Guestrooms have bathrobes, luxury linens, makeup mirrors, and ocean views. http://www.southernmostbeachresort.com/room/la-mer-dewey-ocean-view/.

BEST PET-FRIENDLY

Residence Inn Marriott permits pets 50 pounds or less. There is a nice area for walking dogs, a kitchen area to place dog bowls, and pet owners stay in rooms with doorbells. There is a complimentary breakfast, free parking, laundry facilities, complimentary Wi-Fi, and free shuttle service to the historic downtown area. http://www.marriott.com/hotels/travel/chsri-residence-inn-charleston-downtown-riverview/?pid=corptbta&scid=b661a3c4-9c47-48c8-9e13-75b66089dd79

BEST ROMANTIC HOTEL

The Inn at Middleton Place is adjacent to a plantation and surrounded by live oaks and tall pines. There are fifty-five guestrooms and all rooms have hot tubs, fireplaces, and other amenities.

http://www.theinnatmiddletonplace.com/

BEST HISTORIC HOTEL

Wentworth Mansion was originally built as a private home, circa the 1880s. It is Charleston's only AAA Five Diamond property. Guests enjoy champagne and hor'dourves upon arrival, complimentary breakfast and after dinner drinks (port, sherry, or brandy). You may go up to the rooftop cupola to enjoy an aerial view of the city. Breakfast is served in the carriage house. Their Garden Suites are pet-friendly. There is a spa on site, Urban Nirvana Spa, housed in the old mansion stables. The Wentworth Mansion is within walking distance of downtown Charleston, but is tucked away for peace and quiet.

www.wentworthmansion.com

ABOUT CHARLESTON

There are lots of nicknames for Charleston, including Palmetto City, Holy City, City of Disasters, The Peninsula, City of Firsts, and Silicon Harbor. Charleston is the oldest and second largest city in South Carolina. It was founded in 1670 as Charles Town, in honor of King Charles II. Charleston is one of the most historic cities in America.

The intersection of Meeting and Broad Streets is called the "Four Corners of the Law" because every legal requirement can be done at this junction. On one corner sits St. Michael's Episcopal Church, where couples can get married. On the next corner is the Charleston County Court House, where couples may pay their property taxes. City Hall is located on the next corner, where couples may file for divorce, and on the fourth corner is the post office, where divorced couples may submit change of address forms!

There are 2,800 historically significant buildings in the Charleston area. For a town that is less than 130 square miles, this is remarkable.

One of Charleston's nicknames is "City of Firsts." This is because the first shot of the Civil War was fired in Charleston Harbor at Fort Sumter. The world's first submarine attack occurred here when the *H.L. Hunley* attacked Union warship, *Housatonic*, during a Civil War blockade in 1864.

Our country's first golf course, Harston Green, opened here in 1786. America's first Jockey Club was established here in 1836. More firsts: first historic zoning ordinance (1931), first passenger train (1830), first railway mail service (1831), first prescription drug store (1780), first musical society, St. Cecilia Society (1762), first Chamber of Commerce (1773), first science museum (1773), America's first public museum, Charleston Museum (1773), and the first theatre in America, Dock Street Theatre (1735). The Charleston Museum and Dock Street Theatre still exist today.

The first rice crop ever planted in America was grown on a Charleston plantation. The first female artist to ever be nationally recognized, Henrietta Johnston, was from Charleston.

America's first eminent architect, Robert Mills, was born in Charleston. America's first scientific weather observations took place in Charleston.

The first music store in the U.S. opened on King Street in 1819. The first library in the South opened here in 1748. Charleston is home to the state's first newspaper, *South Carolina Gazette*, in 1732.

And the list goes on and on. Charleston's Eliza Lucas Pinckney was the first to introduce the indigo crop to the U.S. She was the first woman to be inducted into the South Carolina Business Hall of Fame. Her son, Lewis, was the first to grow Sea Island Cotton. From the late 1700s to the early 1900s, Sea Island Cotton was the most important crop and made many planters very wealthy. Reportedly, it was never sold at market because the special cotton blend was so highly sought that French mills contracted it practically before it was planted.

Another nickname is "The Holy City" because there are more churches per capita than anywhere else in North America. Just try to count all the spires and steeples! And they are all significant in one way or another. For example, Beth Elohim is the oldest reform synagogue in the country. The tower bell of St. John's Lutheran Church was melted down to make cannon balls during the Civil War. George Washington attended services at St. Philip's Episcopal Church in 1791.

Many important battles took place in and around Charleston. The city was held by the British during the Revolutionary War from 1780 – 1782. The first clear victory of the Revolutionary War was at Fort Moultrie on nearby Sullivan's Island. Queen Anne's War, King George's War, French and Indian War, Yemasee Indian War, Civil War, World War I, and World War II all had a significant impact on Charleston.

Charleston was where the Ordinance of Secession was voted upon. The greatest damage done to Charleston was during the Civil War. When General Robert E. Lee came to Charleston, two slaves cooking dinner over an open fire accidentally set fire to the city, destroying nearly 550 acres. In 1865, Charleston fell to the Union and citizens set fire to the city rather than relinquish to them. The looting that followed was catastrophic. Priceless heirlooms were stolen by soldiers, officers, and citizens.

Piracy played an important role in Charleston's history. Nefarious and famous pirates, Blackbeard, Stede Bonnet, and others, often raided merchant ships coming and going from this bustling port. Some were hanged at White Point and the Battery.

Mother Nature has taken a tremendous toll with hurricanes, floods, fire, the Great Earthquake of 1886, and the boil weevil, which ended the production of cotton and indigo—the most lucrative crops ever produced here.

It wasn't until the early to mid-1900s that Charleston began to recover from all these events. The U.S. Navy opened a base, and the Charleston Air Force Base opened during WWII. Plantations began producing timber and phosphate instead of cotton and indigo.

More than eight million tons of cargo pass through its port every year, making it the 7th largest cargo port in the U.S. The College of Charleston, the Medical University of South Carolina, and The Citadel are renowned.

However, it is tourism that puts Charleston on the map. It is consistently voted a top destination by TripAdvisor, Conde Nast, Southern Living, Travel & Leisure, Coastal Living, and other media. Roughly nine million visitors come to Charleston annually. It is now considered to be one of the top cruise ports in the United States. Tourism brings in close to $2 billion a year.

FYI: Great Earthquake of 1886 caused significant damage to Charleston Many buildings were destroyed ($5.5 million estimated damage), 100 people died, and it remains the largest recorded earthquake in the southeastern U.S. Charleston lies on a fault line known as the Woodstock Fault, which geologists have determined was caused by a subterranean lava "bloom" that cracked tectonic plates millions of years ago. The adjusting layers caused a severe earthquake in Charleston on August 31, 1886, destroying hundreds of homes throughout the city and damaging many more.

Because of the shaking effect that the earthquake shocks had in knocking down walls in many homes, after that some houses in the city were adorned with metal rods passing through joists and connected by bolts on outer walls. These earthquake bolts can be seen in the form of stars, crosses or round plates on many older homes around Charleston.

ANNUAL EVENTS & AVERAGE TEMPS

There are hundreds of festivals, and special events held year round. Here is a list of some of the biggest and best. For details on these events and a comprehensive list can be found at http://www.charlestoncvb.com/events/.

January

New Year's Celebrations. Charleston hosts many New Year's Eve events, parties, dinners, and celebrations in historic Charleston, SC. The venues and events change annually.

Lowcountry Oyster Festival is all about oysters, but there is music and other food featured.

New Year Polar Swim is held on Sullivan's Island. Brave souls take a quick dip in the Atlantic during this annual charity event.

Southeastern Wildlife Exposition is a three-day celebration of wildlife, including art and wild game culinary events.

February

Mardi Gras and Fat Tuesday Charleston, SC - Each year, during the month of February, Charleston's bars nightclubs, dance clubs, and restaurants get into the spirit. The venues and events change annually.

March

Area Garden Clubs present their annual **Spring Flower Show** at Cypress Gardens.

Artwalk includes up to fifty galleries participating in this amazing annual event.

Kiawah Cup Island Beach Race features the Lowcountry's Marsh Tacky horses.

Charleston Food & Wine Festival celebrates good food and wine with tastings, cooking demonstrations, and special events.

Annual Charleston Antiques Show is a two-day event for serious collectors and amateur enthusiasts.

Festival of Houses & Gardens offers a sneak peek into some of the area's finest homes and their lovely gardens.

Saint Patrick's Day. Many area pubs and restaurants offer special events

<u>April</u>

Blessing of the Fleet and Shrimp Festival is held at Mount Pleasant.

Festival of Houses & Gardens

Cooper River Bridge Run - Register in advance; 40,000+ runners and walkers in this 10K event

Easter. With all the churches in Charleston, Easter is a special time with lots of seasonal events.

Kiawah Island Art & House Tour affords participants a rare glimpse into private homes.

Steeplechase of Charleston is a big, local race held at Stono Ferry.

Blues by the Sea is a music fest

May

Artwalk includes up to fifty galleries participating in a celebration of art.

Charleston Beer Garden is a day of beer, music, and good food.

Spoleto Festival is a decades-old tradition featuring every kind of music, art, theater, and dance.

June

Sweetgrass Cultural Arts Festival is held in nearby Mount Pleasant and is a great way to learn more about the Gullah.

July

4th of July Blast at Patriots Point includes fireworks and a beach theme party.

Charleston Margarita Festival is a competition among restaurants and bars in the greater Charleston area for the best margarita winner.

August

Lowcountry Jazz Festival

BevCon Charleston is all about beverages. Industry professionals gather to have tastings, workshops, and special events.

September

Scottish Games and Highland Gathering is the annual Scottish Games presented by the Charleston Scottish Society.

Southern Living Taste of Charleston

MOJA Arts Festival

October

Artwalk is sponsored by nearly 50 art galleries throughout Charleston.

Taste of Charleston at Boone Hall is sponsored by the Greater Charleston Restaurant Association. Participants can buy tickets and sample food from roughly six dozen different area restaurants. There is a children's area and beer and wine tastings too.

Boone Hall Pumpkin Patch & Maze has all kinds of fall fun for all ages.

Isle of Palms Connector Run

November

Charleston International Film Festival (CIFF) is five days of screenings, special events, music, and the Awards Gala.

Plantation Days at Middleton Place is a weekend long re-creation of plantation days, including cooking, candle making, and other demonstrations.

FYI: ***The most quirky festival award goes to…*** **The Annual Charleston Mac Off! This is the largest macaroni and cheese festival in the country! Believe it or not, this is one of the top things to do in Charleston SC for foodies. More than two dozen restaurants compete in this two-day contest to win bragging rights to the best macaroni and cheese. Participants will enjoy music, kids' activities, and a Demo Kitchen. http://themacoff.com/charleston/**

December

Artwalk includes up to fifty galleries participating in a celebration of art.

Holiday Tour of Homes is a rare chance to see inside some of Charleston's most exclusive residences.

Kiawah Island Golf Resort Marathon

Holiday Festival of Lights James Island County Park is the site of more than a half-million Christmas lights. There is a train ride, marshmallow roast, hot chocolate, Santa's workshop, and more.

Holiday Magic Entertainment & Santa Visits throughout the month of December in downtown Charleston, which is decked out for the holidays. There is storytelling, music, Santa photos, and more. This includes the annual tree lighting ceremony in Marion Square and the annual Christmas Parade that begins at the intersection of Calhoun and Meeting Streets.

Reindeer Run is a 5K in downtown Charleston with prizes for best costumes and more.

North Charleston Christmas Festival kicks off with a tree lighting ceremony and parade. There is music, hayrides, dancing, and more.

Parade of Boats can be seen from Waterfront Park and The Battery. There is a procession of decorated boats that culminates with a fireworks display.

Annual Spirituals Concert is held at Drayton Hall where African-American spiritual music is performed.

Holiday Farmers Market in Marion Square features wreaths, greenery, arts and crafts, and baked goods galore.

FYI: Hurricane Season is June 1 – November 30. From 1990 to 2016, South Carolina has only had five weak tropical cyclone landfalls along the coast: Tropical Storm Kyle in 2002, Hurricane Gaston and Hurricane Charley in 2004, Tropical Storm Ana in 2015, and Tropical Depression Bonnie in 2016.

Average Temps

The best time to visit Charleston is in the spring (March to May) and in the fall (September to November) when temperatures are mild.

Peak tourism is during Easter, Christmas, and summer months, but be forewarned that the Lowcountry is HOT and HUMID during the summer.

Also, this is the Lowcountry, so bugs are prevalent in the summer months.

High °F	Low °F		High °C	Low °C
59	38	January	15	3
63	41	February	17	5
70	47	March	21	8
76	53	April	25	12
83	62	May	28	17
88	70	June	31	21
91	73	July	33	23
90	72	August	32	22
85	67	September	29	20
77	57	October	25	14
70	48	November	21	9
62	40	December	16	5

How to Pack

Charleston is casual for the most part:

*shorts

*sandals/flip flops/beach shoes

*walking shoes

*gear (fishing rod, scuba mask, etc.)

*bathing suit and cover up

*t-shirts

*lightweight pants

*resort casual 'dress' clothes (if plan to dine at upscale restaurant)

*sunscreen and hat

*insect repellent

*rain jacket or windbreaker

*waterproof bag (to safeguard phone, camera, etc.)

*toiletries and cosmetics

*medications

*documents

*batteries, cords and/or chargers

FYI: You can have the best of local Charleston food products delivered to your home once or choose a one-year subscription, www.charlestonepicurean.com.

TERRANCE ZEPKE
Series Reading Order & Guide

Series List

≈

Introduction

Here is a list of titles by Terrance Zepke. They are presented in chronological order although they do not need to be read in any particular order.

Also included is an author bio, a personal message from Terrance, and some other information you may find helpful.

All books are available as eBooks and print books. They can be found on all major booksellers or through your favorite independent bookseller.

For more about this author and her books visit her Author Page at:
http://www.amazon.com/Terrance-Zepke/e/B000APJNIA/.

You can also connect with Terrance on Twitter @terrancezepke or on

www.facebook.com/terrancezepke
www.pinterest.com/terrancezepke
www.goodreads.com/terrancezepke

Sign up for weekly email notifications of the ***Terrance Talks Travel*** blog and receive a FREE 50-page CHEAP TRAVEL REPORT and be the first to learn about new episodes of Uber Adventures, cheap travel tips & resources, and her TRIP PICK OF THE WEEK at www.terrancetalkstravel.com or sign up for her ***Mostly Ghostly*** blog at www.terrancezepke.com.

≈

TERRANCE TALKS TRAVEL

You can follow her travel show, **TERRANCE TALKS TRAVEL: ÜBER ADVENTURES on** www.blogtalkradio.com/terrancetalkstravel or subscribe to it on **iTunes.**

Warning: Listening to this show could lead to a spectacular South African safari, hot-air ballooning over the Swiss Alps, Disney Adventures, and Tornado Tours!

Terrance Zepke is co-host of the writing show, **A WRITER'S JOURNEY: FROM BLANK PAGE TO PUBLISHED.** All episodes can be found on **iTunes** or www.terrancezepke.com.

≈

AUTHOR BIO

Terrance Zepke studied Journalism at the University of Tennessee and later received a Master's degree in Mass Communications from the University of South Carolina. She studied parapsychology at the renowned Rhine Research Center.

Zepke spends much of her time happily traveling around the world but always returns home to the Carolinas where she lives part-time in both states. She has written hundreds of articles and close to three dozen books. She is the host of *Terrance Talks Travel: Über Adventures* and co-host of *A Writer's Journey: From Blank Page to Published.* Additionally, this award-winning and best-selling author has been featured in many publications and programs, such as NPR, CNN, The Washington Post, Associated Press, Travel with Rick Steves, Around the World, Publishers Weekly, World Travel & Dining with Pierre Wolfe, Good Morning Show, The Learning Channel, and The Travel Channel.

When she's not investigating haunted places, searching for pirate treasure, or climbing lighthouses, she is most likely packing for her next adventure to some far flung place, such as Reykjavik or Kwazulu Natal. Some of her favorite adventures include piranha fishing on the Amazon, shark cage diving in South Africa, hiking the Andes Mountains Inca Trail, camping in the Himalayas, dog-sledding in the Arctic Circle, and a gorilla safari in the Congo.

≈

MOST HAUNTED SERIES

A Ghost Hunter's Guide to the Most Haunted Places in America (2012)
https://read.amazon.com/kp/embed?asin=B0085SG22O&preview=newtab&linkCode=kpe&ref_=cm_sw_r_kb_dp_zerQwb1AMJ0R4

A Ghost Hunter's Guide to the Most Haunted Houses in America (2013)
https://read.amazon.com/kp/embed?asin=B00C3PUMGC&preview=newtab&linkCode=kpe&ref_=cm_sw_r_kb_dp_BfrQwb1WF1Y6T

A Ghost Hunter's Guide to the Most Haunted Hotels & Inns in America (2014)
https://read.amazon.com/kp/embed?asin=B00C3PUMGC&preview=newtab&linkCode=kpe

A Ghost Hunter's Guide to the Most Haunted Historic Sites in America (2016)

https://read.amazon.com/kp/embed?asin=B01LXADK90&preview=newtab&linkCode=kpe&ref_=cm_sw_r_kb_dp_WFFLybJ2TWGAR

TERRANCE TALKS TRAVEL: The Quirky Tourist Guide to Charleston, South Carolina | Terrance Zepke

The Ghost Hunter's MOST HAUNTED Box Set (3 in 1): Discover America's Most Haunted Destinations (2016)

https://read.amazon.com/kp/embed?asin=B01HISAAJM&preview=newtab&linkCode=kpe&ref_=cm_sw_r_kb_dp_AGFLybMNFJKBA

MOST HAUNTED and SPOOKIEST Sampler Box Set: Featuring *A GHOST HUNTER'S GUIDE TO THE MOST HAUNTED PLACES IN AMERICA* and *SPOOKIEST CEMETERIES* (2017)

https://read.amazon.com/kp/embed?asin=B01N17EEOM&preview=newtab&linkCode=kpe&ref_=cm_sw_r_kb_dp_.JFLybCTN3QEF

A Ghost Hunter's Guide to the Most Haunted Places in the World (2018)
https://read.amazon.com/kp/embed?asin=B078ZL382D&preview=newtab&linkCode=kpe&ref_=cm_sw_r_kb_dp_nVNXAb61HF42W

≈

TERRANCE TALKS TRAVEL SERIES

Terrance Talks Travel: A Pocket Guide to South Africa (2015)
https://read.amazon.com/kp/embed?asin=B00PSTFTLI&preview=newtab&linkCode=kpe&ref_=cm_sw_r_kb_dp_pirQwb12XZX65

Terrance Talks Travel: A Pocket Guide to African Safaris (2015)
https://read.amazon.com/kp/embed?asin=B00PSTFZSA&preview=newtab&linkCode=kpe&ref_=cm_sw_r_kb_dp_jhrQwb0P8Z87G

Terrance Talks Travel: A Pocket Guide to Adventure Travel (2015)
https://read.amazon.com/kp/embed?asin=B00UKMAVQG&preview=newtab&linkCode=kpe&ref_=cm_sw_r_kb_dp_ThrQwb1PVVZAZ

Terrance Talks Travel: A Pocket Guide to Florida Keys (including Key West & The Everglades) (2016)
https://read.amazon.com/kp/embed?asin=B01EWHML58&preview=newtab&linkCode=kpe&ref_=cm_sw_r_kb_dp_YMbHybP0ZZEFK

Terrance Talks Travel: The Quirky Tourist Guide to Key West (2017)

https://read.amazon.com/kp/embed?asin=B01N3BF80O&preview=newtab&linkCode=kpe&ref_=cm_sw_r_kb_dp_wHFLyb1F89GNR

Terrance Talks Travel: The Quirky Tourist Guide to Cape Town (2017)

https://read.amazon.com/kp/embed?asin=B01N6YKI77&preview=newtab&linkCode=kpe&ref_=cm_sw_r_kb_dp_jIFLybNCTJ5NN

African Safari Box Set: Featuring TERRANCE TALKS TRAVEL: *A Pocket Guide to South Africa* and *TERRANCE TALKS TRAVEL: A Pocket Guide to African Safaris* (2017)
https://read.amazon.com/kp/embed?asin=B01MUH6VJU&preview=newtab&linkCode=kpe&ref_=cm_sw_r_kb_dp_xLFLybAQKFA0B

Terrance Talks Travel: The Quirky Tourist Guide to Reykjavik (2017)
https://www.amazon.com/Terrance-Zepke/e/B000APJNIA/ref=sr_ntt_srch_lnk_15?qid=1488514258&sr=8-15

Terrance Talks Travel: The Quirky Tourist Guide to Charleston, South Carolina (2017)
https://www.amazon.com/Terrance-Zepke/e/B000APJNIA/ref=sr_ntt_srch_lnk_15?qid=1488514258&sr=8-15

Terrance Talks Travel: The Quirky Tourist Guide to Ushuaia (2017) https://www.amazon.com/Terrance-Zepke/e/B000APJNIA/ref=sr_ntt_srch_lnk_15?qid=1488514258&sr=8-15

Terrance Talks Travel: The Quirky Tourist Guide to Antarctica (2017) https://www.amazon.com/Terrance-Zepke/e/B000APJNIA/ref=sr_ntt_srch_lnk_1?qid=1489092624&sr=8-1

TERRANCE TALKS TRAVEL: The Quirky Tourist Guide to Machu Picchu & Cuzco (Peru) 2017 https://read.amazon.com/kp/embed?asin=B07147HLQY&preview=newtab&linkCode=kpe&ref_=cm_sw_r_kb_dp_HmZmzb9FT5E0P

Terrance Talks Travel: A Pocket Guide to East Africa's Uganda and Rwanda (2018) https://read.amazon.com/kp/embed?asin=B079YN892B&preview=newtab&linkCode=kpe&ref_=cm_sw_r_kb_dp_RWvQAbR3KQVQM

TERRANCE TALKS TRAVEL: The Quirky Tourist Guide to Kathmandu (Nepal) & The Himalayas (2018) https://www.amazon.com/Terrance-Zepke/e/B000APJNIA/ref=dp_byline_cont_ebooks_1

TERRANCE TALKS TRAVEL: The Quirky Tourist Guide to Charleston, South Carolina | Terrance Zepke

African Safari Box Set: Featuring TERRANCE TALKS TRAVEL: *A Pocket Guide to South Africa* and *TERRANCE TALKS TRAVEL: A Pocket Guide to African Safaris* (2017)
https://read.amazon.com/kp/embed?asin=B01MUH6VJU&preview=newtab&linkCode=kpe&ref_=cm_sw_r_kb_dp_xLFLybAQKFA0B

≈

CHEAP TRAVEL SERIES

How to Cruise Cheap! (2017)

https://read.amazon.com/kp/embed?asin=B01N6NYM1N&preview=newtab&linkCode=kpe&ref_=cm_sw_r_kb_dp_6DFLybR27HH38

How to Fly Cheap! (2017)

https://read.amazon.com/kp/embed?asin=B01N7Q81YG&preview=newtab&linkCode=kpe&ref_=cm_sw_r_kb_dp_5EFLybR6GNNHD

How to Travel Cheap! (2017)

https://www.amazon.com/Terrance-Zepke/e/B000APJNIA/

How to Travel FREE or Get Paid to Travel! (2017)

https://www.amazon.com/Terrance-Zepke/e/B000APJNIA/

CHEAP TRAVEL SERIES (4 IN 1) BOX SET (2017)
https://read.amazon.com/kp/embed?asin=B071ZGV1TY&preview=newtab&linkCode=kpe&ref_=cm_sw_r_kb_dp_.VNXAb8HMFQDY

≈

SPOOKIEST SERIES

Spookiest Lighthouses (2013)
https://read.amazon.com/kp/embed?asin=B00EAAQA2S&preview

Spookiest Battlefields (2015)
https://read.amazon.com/kp/embed?asin=B00XUSWS3G&preview=newtab&linkCode=kpe&ref_=cm_sw_r_kb_dp_okrQwb0TR9F8M

Spookiest Cemeteries (2016)

https://read.amazon.com/kp/embed?asin=B01D0FP498&preview=newtab&linkCode=kpe&ref_=cm_sw_r_kb_dp_wJFLyb3X9XSK7

Spookiest Box Set (3 in 1): Discover America's Most Haunted Destinations (2016)
https://read.amazon.com/kp/embed?asin=B01HH2OM4I&preview=newtab&linkCode=kpe&ref_=cm_sw_r_kb_dp_Anz-xbT3SDEZS

MOST HAUNTED and SPOOKIEST Sampler Box Set: Featuring *A GHOST HUNTER'S GUIDE TO THE MOST HAUNTED PLACES IN AMERICA* and *SPOOKIEST CEMETERIES* (2017)

https://read.amazon.com/kp/embed?asin=B01N17EEOM&preview=newtab&linkCode=kpe&ref_=cm_sw_r_kb_dp_.JFLybCTN3QEF

Spookiest Objects (2017)
https://read.amazon.com/kp/embed?asin=B0728FMVZF&preview=newtab&linkCode=kpe&ref_=cm_sw_r_kb_dp_TXNXAbS0DF352

≈

STOP TALKING SERIES

Stop Talking & Start Writing Your Book (2015)
https://read.amazon.com/kp/embed?asin=B012YHTIAY&preview=newtab&linkCode=kpe&ref_=cm_sw_r_kb_dp_qlrQwb1N7G3YF

Stop Talking & Start Publishing Your Book (2015)
https://read.amazon.com/kp/embed?asin=B013HHV1LE&preview=newtab&linkCode=kpe&ref_=cm_sw_r_kb_dp_WlrQwb1F63MFD

Stop Talking & Start Selling Your Book (2015)
https://read.amazon.com/kp/embed?asin=B015YAO33K&preview=newtab&linkCode=kpe&ref_=cm_sw_r_kb_dp_ZkrQwb188J8BE

Stop Talking & Start Writing Your Book Series (3 in 1) Box Set (2016)

https://read.amazon.com/kp/embed?asin=B01M58J5AZ&preview=newtab&linkCode=kpe&ref_=cm_sw_r_kb_dp_4MFLybYA8CP9F

≈

CAROLINAS FOR KIDS SERIES

Lighthouses of the Carolinas for Kids (2009)
http://www.amazon.com/Lighthouses-Carolinas-Kids-Terrance-Zepke/dp/1561644293/ref=asap_bc?ie=UTF8

Pirates of the Carolinas for Kids (2009)
https://read.amazon.com/kp/embed?asin=B01BJ3VSWK&preview=newtab&linkCode=kpe&ref_=cm_sw_r_kb_dp_rGrXwb0XDTSTA

Ghosts of the Carolinas for Kids (2011)
https://read.amazon.com/kp/embed?asin=B01BJ3VSVQ&preview=newtab&linkCode=kpe&ref_=cm_sw_r_kb_dp_XLrXwb0E7N1AK

≈

GHOSTS OF THE CAROLINAS SERIES

Ghosts of the Carolina Coasts (1999)
http://www.amazon.com/Ghosts-Carolina-Coasts-Terrance-Zepke/dp/1561641758/ref=asap_bc?ie=UTF8

The Best Ghost Tales of South Carolina (2004)
http://www.amazon.com/Best-Ghost-Tales-South-Carolina/dp/1561643068/ref=asap_bc?ie=UTF8

Ghosts & Legends of the Carolina Coasts (2005)
https://read.amazon.com/kp/embed?asin=B01AGQJABW&preview=newtab&linkCode=kpe&ref_=cm_sw_r_kb_dp_VKrXwb1Q09794

The Best Ghost Tales of North Carolina (2006)
https://read.amazon.com/kp/embed?asin=B01BJ3VSV6&preview=newtab&linkCode=kpe&ref_=cm_sw_r_kb_dp_6IrXwb0XKT90Q

≈

BOOKS & GUIDES FOR THE CAROLINAS SERIES

Pirates of the Carolinas (2005)
http://www.amazon.com/Pirates-Carolinas-Terrance-Zepke/dp/1561643440/ref=asap_bc?ie=UTF8

Coastal South Carolina: Welcome to the Lowcountry (2006)
http://www.amazon.com/Coastal-South-Carolina-Welcome-Lowcountry/dp/1561643483/ref=asap_bc?ie=UTF8

Coastal North Carolina: Its Enchanting Islands, Towns & Communities (2011)
http://www.amazon.com/Coastal-North-Carolina-Terrance-Zepke/dp/1561645117/ref=asap_bc?ie=UTF8

Lighthouses of the Carolinas: A Short History & Guide (2011)
https://read.amazon.com/kp/embed?asin=B01AGQJA7G&preview=newtab&linkCode=kpe&ref_=cm_sw_r_kb_dp_UHrXwb09A22P1

≈

MORE BOOKS BY TERRANCE ZEPKE

Lowcountry Voodoo: Tales, Spells & Boo Hags (2009)
https://read.amazon.com/kp/embed?asin=B018WAGUC6&preview=newtab&linkCode=kpe&ref_=cm_sw_r_kb_dp_UmrQwb19AVSYG

Ghosts of Savannah (2012)
http://www.amazon.com/Ghosts-Savannah-Terrance-Zepke/dp/1561645303/ref=asap_bc?ie=UTF8

How To Train Your Puppy or Dog Using Three Simple Strategies (FUN & FAST!) (2017)
https://read.amazon.com/kp/embed?asin=B01MZ5GN2M&preview=newtab&linkCode=kpe&ref_=cm_sw_r_kb_dp_bQFLyb76G2KYW

*Fiction books were written under a pseudonym.

≈

Message from the Author

The primary purpose of this guide is to introduce you to some titles you may not have known about. Another reason for it is to let you know all the ways you can connect with me. Authors love to hear from readers. We truly appreciate you more than you'll ever know. Please feel free to send me a comment or question via the comment form found on every page on www.terrancezepke.com and www.terrancetalkstravel.com or follow me on your favorite social media. Don't forget that you can also listen to my writing podcast on iTunes, **A Writer's Journey**, or my travel show, **Terrance Talks Travel: Über Adventures** on Blog Talk Radio and iTunes. The best way to make sure you don't miss any episodes of these shows (and find a complete archive of shows), new book releases and giveaways, contests, my TRIP PICK OF THE WEEK, cheap travel tips, free downloadable travel reports, and more is to subscribe to ***Terrance Talks Travel*** on www.terrancetalkstravel.com or ***Mostly Ghostly*** on www.terrancezepke.com. If you'd like to learn more about any of my books, you can find in-depth descriptions and "look inside" options through most online booksellers. Also, please note that links to book previews have been included in SERIES section of this booklet for your convenience.

Thank you for your interest and HAPPY READING!

Terrance

INDEX

A

B

C

D

E

F

G

H

I

J

K

L

M

R

S

T

U

W

Made in the USA
Middletown, DE
23 April 2019